Fake News in Real Co

by Paul Levinson

Copyright 2016-2017 by Paul Levinson
ISBN 978-1-56178-054-9
Photograph on book cover by Paul Levinson
Published by Connected Editions, Inc.

Table of Contents

Government Media vs. Independent Press
Citizen Journalism
Propaganda and Persuasion
Fake News
Crying Fake News and "Alternative Facts"
Remedies for Fake News

Bibliography
About the Author

Fake news -- or news in which falsities appear by deliberate intent rather than accident or error -- has reared its head in the recent 2016 U. S. Presidential election, has been cited as one of the causes of its result, and continues to make headlines in real news reports. Fake news received 8.7 million "engagements" (likes or other reactions, shares, and comments) in comparison to 7.3 million for real news on Facebook between February 2016 and Election Day on November 7, 2016, with the biggest increase right before the election (Lee, 2016). Hillary Clinton denounced "the epidemic of malicious fake news" in a post-election speech on December 8, 2016 as "a danger that must be addressed," adding that "fake news isn't about partisanship or politics, lives are at risk" (Clinton, 2016). She was no doubt referring to a man who walked into the Comet Ping Pong pizzeria in Washington, DC and pointed a gun, under the delusion that there was a child predation ring at work in the restaurant, having read in fake news stories that Hillary and Bill Clinton, and Anthony Weiner, were pursuing pedophilic interests in the pizza place (see Gillin, 2016, for further details). There's almost something science fictional about this, except in The Man in the High Castle (Dick, 1962 & Spotnitz, 2015/2016; see Levinson, 2016b, for review of the television series), the fake news stories are real in an alternate reality (ours). And fake news is no longer just an American problem, as former U. N. Secretary-General Ban Ki-moon demonstrated, when he cited "fake news" stories about him as the reason for abruptly deciding not to run for President of South Korea (Fifield, 2017), at the beginning of February 2017. The German cabinet in April 2017 already has drafted a bill, deemed likely to be enacted, that would levy hefty fines on sites such as Facebook and Twitter that publish fake news (Faiola & Kirchner, 2017).

What follows is a brief attempt to put fake news in historical and current context -- compare it to government controlled, non-government professional, and citizen journalism -- and identify its best remedies.

Government Media versus Independent Press

Professional journalism as we know it in its various forms - ranging from print in The New York Times to broadcasting on the BBC and CNN to news on the Internet in The Huffington Post - is a relatively recent phenomenon in the world, and was a consequence of the printing press in Europe, introduced by Gutenberg about half a century before Columbus sailed across the Atlantic.

Printing presses back then were very costly to construct and operate, and monarchs were the only ones who could easily afford them. The mercantile class, however, empowered by the very spread of commercial information disseminated by the new presses, soon provided an alternative to royal presses. The independent press emerged, supported by advertising rather than royal purses, and loyal to no one, in principle, other than the pursuit of truth.

In the United States, this independence has been famously supported, enforced, and embodied in the First Amendment (ratified in 1791) to the Constitution, and its stricture that "Congress shall make no law ... abridging the freedom of speech, or of the press". And although this amendment has been battered on a variety of fronts -- most significantly in the U. S. Supreme Court "Schenck v the United States" decision in 1919 that some kinds of communication, such as falsely shouting fire in a crowded theater, ought not be protected from government restriction and prosecution, and by the Federal Communications Act of 1934, which regulates broadcasting -- the First Amendment has been respected and even extended in many ways, including in the Supreme Court's 1997 decision in "Reno v the American Civil Liberties Union" that expression of political opinion on the Internet is entitled to the same protection as its expression in newsprint.

At the same time, the notion of the press as properly an organ and exponent of government grew in the 20th century in totalitarian states such as Nazi Germany and the Soviet Union, and continues to some extent to this very day in Russia, China, and lesser dictatorial states around the world. Indeed, the view that the public is best served by a press that supports the government and justifies its policies has roots as far back as Ancient Athens, and the view of Plato that some forms of communication such as poetry should be restricted because their adverse effects on the intellect, in contrast to the teachings of his mentor Socrates who wanted to maximize dialogue (see Popper, 1945, for Plato's philosophy as a foundation of totalitarian 20th century governments). This schism continued through history, in the conflict between Galileo and the Roman Catholic Church, and even in the founding of the United States, with John Adams wanting a press that was uncritical of the government, in stark contrast to Thomas Jefferson and the other drafters of the First Amendment. (The best book about this is Tedford & Herbeck, 2013; see also Levinson, 2005).

The goal and raison d'etre of a free press was and is to seek out and report the truth, whether it is critical or supportive of the government. That activity -- honest reporting of the facts and the truth -- is precisely what the First Amendment is supposed to protect. Of course, since reporters are human beings, they are bound to make mistakes on occasion. To identify and root out such inevitable errors, the professional press puts into the field of journalism a variety of procedures prior to publication, including fact-checking and insistence on more than one reliable source. Indeed, the professional press could be defined as pursuit of the truth, with the pursuit safeguarded by time-honored techniques to insure that it is the truth not a falsity which is being reported.

Nonetheless, since not only the reporters but the fact-checkers and editors in professional media are after all only human and inevitably imperfect, errors do get through the gates, as attested to by the "errata" listed at the bottom of the front page of The New York Times, and apologies heard all too often on cable news. As an instructive example, I was correctly quoted in a recent article in The Christian Science Monitor (Reilly, 2017) about fake news, of all topics, but my name was misspelled as "Saul":

> After all, sites with fake news are only catering to their audiences. Saul Levinson, a communications professor at Fordham University in New York, told the Monitor in December that, "These bubbles have not been imposed upon the public – it was what the people want. As long as social media continues to provide a very easy forum for these news bubbles ... it is not going to stop."

A colleague noticed the error, notified me, and I turn sent a Tweet about it the writer.   The error was corrected with an hour:

> After all, sites with fake news are only catering to their audiences. Paul Levinson, a communications professor at Fordham University in New York, told the Monitor in December that, "These bubbles have not been imposed upon the public – it was what the people want. As long as social media continues to provide a very easy forum for these news bubbles ... it is not going to stop." [**Editor's note:** *An earlier version of this story misspelled Mr. Levinson's first name.*]

And on the rare occasions when a journalist deliberately concocts deceptions instead of reporting news, the professional press publishes detailed, high-profile apologies and explanations, as The New York Times did when it discovered in 2003 what its reporter Jayson Blair had been doing on its pages (Barry et al, 2003).

Professional journalism could be better defined, therefore, as an honest attempt to find and report the truth, safeguarded by an honest attempt to identify and eliminate errors, via people and processes independent of the reporter. A key word here in both parts of the definition is "attempt," since all of these processes are imperfect, and errors do succeed in slipping through these gatekeepers and out to the public.

Further, it is certainly not the case that everything that appears on newspaper pages, or is spoken or shown on radio and television, is intended to be factual and true. The essence of advertising, on which all of our free press depends, is not to inform but persuade, in particular about the excellence of the product or cause being promoted, and this inevitably entails exaggeration, and/or omission of pertinent facts, which is otherwise known as deception. News media partake of such an approach even in their self-advertising or mottos. The New York Times daily informs us on the top of its front page that it is providing "All the News That's Fit to Print," in contrast to what the Times is really offering readers, which could be more truthfully described as "all the news that the editors of The New York Times deem fit to print".

But unlike fake news, which poses as truth and apparently succeeds on occasion, advertising in traditional media is usually obviously advertising, and is able to convince and motivate the public without pretending to be news. The price we literally pay for a free press -- ads encouraging us to buy products, including newspapers, or watch this or that news show on television, or vote for this or that political candidate – is thus not so steep as to make our free media less preferable to the alternative of a press controlled by government.

And should a slogan or ad be presented in such a way as to make it indistinguishable from news, we have the same defense as we have for the stubborn errors that might accidentally get past an editor or fact-checker: the public itself. Which brings us to citizen journalism.

Citizen Journalism

Even in Jefferson's day, anyone could be a reporter in terms of discovering and writing about newsworthy events. But in order for that reporting to be accessible by the general public, a printing press and a newspaper were needed -- i.e., a professional press.

As Marshall McLuhan (1977) noted long before the advent of social media, photocopying machines were already giving every author a means of publication. But photocopied pages were cumbersome in comparison to newspapers, and looked nothing like them.

The Internet, and in particular social media and their capacity to make every consumer a producer (Levinson, 2009/2013), changed all of that. There's much less difference between what *The New York Times* and a blog looks like online, than there is between *The New York Times* and a xeroxed manuscript. In addition, smartphones soon gave everyone in the public the ready and easy means to be a photojournalist and a videographer.

The question almost immediately arose as to whether citizen journalists were entitled to the same First Amendment protections as professional journalists. Authorities at all levels of state, local, and Federal government, already chafing under First Amendment protections for establishment media, were all too happy to proceed on the basis of none being afforded to self-proclaimed journalists using blogs and websites as their means of publication. Josh Wolf was sent to prison for not revealing the sources of his videos in his coverage of G-8 Summit in San Francisco in 2006, where a police officer was assaulted. But the "shield law" to which Wolf claimed entitlement -- the option of journalists not to reveal their sources when so ordered by a judge -- had not been established on a national level (and still is not) even for professional journalists, so Wolf's case entailed issues which went beyond citizen journalism. He was held in contempt of court and put in jail, but was released eight months later, after prosecutors decided his evidence was no longer needed. An example more directly related to the First Amendment and citizen journalists arose a few years later in the Occupy Wall Street protests in New York City in 2011, where Alexander Arbuckle was arrested for "blocking traffic" when he was reporting about a demonstration as a citizen journalist. He was subsequently found "not guilty," mainly due to the evidence of another citizen journalist, Tim Pool, who had video-recorded the activity in the street at the time of Arbuckle's arrest (see Levinson 2009/2013 for details), and showed that Arbuckle was not blocking anything -- except perhaps the equanimity of then Mayor Michael Bloomberg of New York, who was no friend of Occupy Wall Street.

Regarding the goal or motivation of citizen journalists and reporting the truth, there is no difference between them and professional journalists: both want to convey the truth to the public. The difference resides in the lack of institutional safeguards for making sure that citizen journalists are indeed reporting the truth. They are certainly free to fact-check on their own, but fact-checking one's own work is usually not as effective as fact-checking by someone other than the reporter, and usually the only customs in citizen journalism about how many sources are needed to confirm the veracity of a story are supplied, again, by the citizen journalist herself or himself. On the other hand, there are obvious advantages to citizen journalism, such as being immediately on the scene of an important, breaking news event, and being able to report it immediately, given the ubiquity and communicative power of smartphones.

Potential errors in citizen journalism are discoverable by the same ultimate method for calling out errors which survive the institutional checks in professional journalism: the general public. Here it is worth noting the study done by Nature magazine in 2005 about the level of errors in the Encyclopedia Britannica, the archetypical professional encyclopedia, and those found on Wikipedia, written completely by readers certified only by the fact that they are human beings. The study (Giles, 2005) found no significant difference in the number of errors. Why was this? The crowd-sourced error correction on Wikipedia worked as effectively as the expert vetting of all articles in the Encyclopedia Britannica.

Moreover, Wikipedia readers are encouraged to correct errors, and this may be exactly at work with the Web-conversant public regarding professionally unchecked citizen journalism: if not correcting errors in citizen journalism, discovering them, via recourse to easily accessible, multiple sources on the Internet.

But that same ease also facilitates the dissemination of deception.

Propaganda and Persuasion

Unlike news, whether conveyed by professional reporters or citizen journalists, the purpose of propaganda is not to inform but sway. As such, news media controlled by government are usually engaged in propaganda -- make the government and its policies look good -- rather than reporting facts. But propaganda has also been and continues to be a central feature of democracies with robust, independent news media. The difference between propaganda in totalitarian versus free societies is that propaganda masquerades as truth and fact when produced by government-controlled media, and thus is a kind of fake news, unlike propaganda in open societies, where it is usually clearly discernible from reporting of news.

But propaganda uses the same operating principles, whether its purpose is good or bad, whether in states with government-controlled media or a free press. Public service ads, commercials for chewing gum, political campaigns, religious teachings, education, and interpersonal relations are all propaganda or partake of propaganda in democratic societies, because the primary or subsidiary purpose of such communication is to influence, convince, and persuade. Since the late 1930s, the Institute for Propaganda Analysis (Lee & Lee, 1939) and other organizations and researchers have identified prominent types of propaganda employed in diverse aspects of life in all societies. These include "testimonial" or "appeal to authority" (think or do something because someone presumably in a position to know more or better than you urges you to have that opinion or take that action), "just plain folks" (think or do something because everyone else is doing it), "scapegoating" (blame an ill on a convenient target), etc. (Some critics of the modern age, such as Jacques Ellul, 1962, have argued that everything conveyed by technology is inherently distortive or propagandistic, but such a view is self-refuting, insofar as it was presented in a product of technology, a book produced by a printing press.)

Significantly, propaganda does not abhor or even necessarily avoid the truth. But it is presented only to the extent that it serves the larger purpose of persuading rather than informing. Thus, an appeal to authority may accurately provide the analysis of someone who indeed may better informed on the topic at hand than are you, but the purpose of such an appeal is to short-circuit your own analysis and pre-empt your own logic and instead accept on face value the testimony of the expert.

This appeal to emotion is also the essence of fake news, which goes one big step further than appeal-to-authority propaganda, by making recipients feel they are now authorities on the subject, by virtue of the false news that they have received about it.

Fake News

In contrast to both professional journalism and citizen journalism, fake news has no goal of reporting the truth. Indeed, errors or divergences from the truth happen in fake news not by inadvertence or mistake, but because those errors are what purveyors of fake news want to convey.

In that sense, fake news shares a motive with governmental controlled media, designed not to convey the truth, but support the government, whether such support coincides with the truth or not. And when the truth is specifically at variance with governmental policy, the government's vehicles of news are deliberately tasked with providing stories which are not true. A relatively recent example, with almost comical overtones, would be Mohammed Saeed al-Sahhaf, aka "Baghdad Bob," who as Iraqi Information Minister in 2003 reported great daily victories for the Iraqis as American-lead coalition forces were entering Baghdad in the final phases of the war (see Harmon, 2003, for details). More sinister was the KGB's long campaign of "disinformation" aka fake news against the United States, including spreading word that AIDS was germ-warfare gone wrong by the U. S., and the CIA was behind JFK's assassination (so effective was the latter that many still believe this). To make matters even more complicated and situated on the razor's edge of you don't know whether to laugh or cry, the BBC (Corera, 2017) published an article about KGB fake news on April 1 -- or April Fool's Day, the de facto official day in which fake news of the ridiculous kind is supposed to be disseminated.

But fake news is deadly serious, and though it shares the wellspring of the digital revolution which makes possible citizen journalism, it also closes a loop and returns to a form of "news" which predates even traditional, professional journalism and the free press. In fact, fake news as a hazard to the mass public goes back as far as the printing press in Europe (see Soll, 2016, for some choice examples). Photography, certainly a more objective recording of reality than painting and a staple of news media, has been doctored since its inception in the 1840s (Metropolitan Museum of Art, 2012), a practice which has become commonplace with Photoshop. The following is a classic example, in which Abraham Lincoln's head was swapped in for John C. Calhoun's, because there were no heroic poses of the President on hand in the 1860s (Selwyn-Holmes, 2010):

As McLuhan might well have put this, fake news "retrieves" the severance from truth which typified government propaganda and news in general in pre-democratic monarchies and subsequent totalitarian or otherwise non-democratic states, characterized some reporting in democracies as well, and still does in all countries (see Levinson, 2015/2016, for more on McLuhan's concept of "retrieval" in his "tetradic" or four-part assessment of the effects of media, and an application of that intellectual tool towards understanding social media).

But for most of the 575 years between Gutenberg's printing press and today's social media, there was a ready remedy for fake news. As Hugo Gernsback pointed out in 1926, about a series of articles published in The New York Sun in 1835 claiming that intelligent life had been discovered on the Moon, "such a hoax ... today ... would not last twenty-four hours, because verification or denial would speedily be brought about" by radio (see Wythoff, 2016, for more). Orson Welles' "War of the Worlds" 1938 radio broadcast soon provided at least one famous refutation of Gernsback's confidence in radio, and in the todays of 2016 and 2017, social media not only speedily refute fake news, but are the prime engines of its dissemination.

Thus, fake news has become an omnipresent candidate for reporting by non-fake news media, social and traditional, as an example of the breakdown of our society, at the same time as social media just a click away continue to spread deceptions. Fake news is in the air, on the air in traditional broadcast and cable media, and on the verge of achieving iconic status as a metaphor or straightforward explanation even for phenomena that were never news in the first place. A recent commentator (Livingston, 2016) wondered if the appearance of Peter Cushing (who died in 1994) in live action in the new Star Wars movie Rogue One via digital artistry wasn't "a small step to the 'false news' we hear so much about in politics". I have been somewhat guilty of this myself, in a different way, observing that the Science and Security Board of the Bulletin of the Atomic Scientists (2017) movement of the "Doomsday Clock" forward 30 seconds bore some resemblance to fake news, not because there was anything untrue about the announcement, but because the implication that this "Clock" has any real numerical or scientific connection to the future of the world -- backed by actual data as in the case of climate change, for example -- was untrue, and an example of appeal-to-authority propaganda (Levinson, 2017a).

Fake news does have much in common with propaganda -- governmental, scientific, and personal -- and if reports are true that the dissemination of at least some fake news stories was amplified by Russian "bots," with the intention of assisting Donald Trump in the 2016 U.S. Presidential election (see, Dougherty, 2016, for a summary), then the connection between fake news and government propaganda is not only theoretical and metaphoric, but about as real-politic as it gets. But there is also a second, very different kind of motive behind fake news, which puts it in league with professional journalism and citizen journalism some of the time: the pursuit of money. As Jacob Soboroff's (2016) interview for MSNBC (a professional news medium) with Jestin Coler (a disseminator of fake news) makes abundantly clear, the purpose of that fake news was to generate income, via attracting viewers to the fake news site. Ironically, that is the same purpose of MSNBC and all professional news operations, in print, on radio and television, and on the Web. Also ironically, Coler says he voted for Clinton, and regrets what his fake news site may have wrought in her losing the electoral college vote, and therein the Presidential election.   (See also Smith & Banic, 2016, and their interview with a creator of fake news stories, who lives in Macedonia, is 18-years old, and says he earned $60,000 from clicks on advertising on bogus news stories that generated more than 40 million views.)

Since professional journalism in print, broadcasting, cable, and the Web is far more governed by pursuit of money, in the need to make corporate profit, than is citizen journalism, usually practiced by individuals for whom monetary profit is not the main motive or any motive at all, or the goal is a relatively small amount of money needed by an individual in contrast to corporate sums needed to satisfy stockholders, professional journalism has more in common with fake news than does citizen journalism. On the other hand, professional journalists have been diligent and quick and eager to investigate fake news and bring it to the public's attention, as indeed they should (see again, for example, Dougherty, 2016 and Soboroff, 2016, and there are numerous others).

But what role, then, did fake news play in determining the results of the American election? Hillary Clinton provided a persuasive and well-informed argument that fake news was in part responsible for her losing the election (in the Electoral College) in an interview by Kara Swisher and Walt Mossberg on May 31, 2017, correctly identifying the "personal" delivery of "lies" about her -- i. e., via social media -- as especially effective (Farnsworth, 2017). But learning why people voted one way or the other is always a dicey, unreliable proposition, since there is no way of knowing if people are telling the truth when they're polled for their voting motives.   But since Hillary Clinton won the popular vote by nearly three million more votes, attributing her loss to fake news would be a steep climb. Indeed, the vote totals in the 2016 U. S. Presidential election support Thomas Jefferson's view, derived from John Milton, that, given a choice of truth versus falsity, or, in today's parlance, true news versus false news, a majority of people recognized the truth. (See Percival, 2011, for the resilience of rationality to diverse modes of deception.) Anyone wanting to contend otherwise, let alone prove that fake news was decisive in the election, would need to demonstrate why fake news had a special effect in states that Hillary Clinton narrowly lost -- such as Pennsylvania, Michigan, and Wisconsin -- but not narrowly won, or won by huge margins, such as New York and California (but see Stone & Gordon, 2017, for some preliminary indications that Russian-created fake news may have targeted swing state voters in the Midwest). Indeed, that would be a challenge for proof that any single factor was decisive -- such as FBI Director James Comey stirring up Clinton's email controversy, in violation of FBI policy not to make statements that could influence elections so close to their occurrence (see Chozick, 2016) -- unless that factor had some special relevance to the states that Hillary lost (which perhaps would be the case for the "rust-belt" Midwestern states if the factor cited was her lack of appeal to workers displaced by the digital revolution).

Whatever its impact on the 2016 Presidential election, fake news goes hand-in-hand (or maybe finger-to-keypad) with another new phenomenon of the digital age, so-called "news bubbles," or the propensity of people to seek out on the Web the views that most agree with what they already most believe. This characteristic of human nature vastly precedes the Internet. Leon Festinger's (1957) theory of "cognitive dissonance," or the tendency of people to avoid ideas which conflict with their core beliefs, goes back to the mid-20th century, as does McLuhan's (1964) notion of "narcissus narcosis," or the fondness we have for reflections of our own ideas and feelings in the media we encounter. Both effects are more commonly known in the 21st century as "confirmation bias" or "congeniality bias" (see Hart et al, 2009). McLuhan went further and thought we were all in danger of ending up like the youth Narcissus of Greek mythology, so vain and in love with his own reflection in the water that he reached into it and drowned, despite all manner of attractive entreaties from a nearby nymph. (There are several versions of the story, but this is the one that most immediately occurred to me, because its lesson is so literally at hand and a splash in the face.) Taking refuge in what comforts us is also what McLuhan (1970) was getting at when he noted that ads provide the good news to balance the bad news in television news shows, a pattern which also resulted in HGTV and its portrayal of beautiful homes attracting more viewers than CNN in 2016 (Smith, 2016).

Crying Fake News and "Alternative Facts"

But do people necessarily believe and act upon what they encounter in fake news, when that coincides with and affirms what they already hold to be true? We need to keep returning to that question, because its answer will tell us to what extent fake news is in fact a public menace rather than a media concern or an excuse for losing an election. Indeed, speaking of fake news being used as an excuse -- or what we might call "crying fake news" -- Donald Trump was quick to denounce unverified reports of the Russians seeking to potentially blackmail him with recordings of sexual perversions when he was in Moscow as "FAKE NEWS - A TOTAL POLITICAL WITCH HUNT!" (all caps in Tweet from Trump, see Beech, 2017), which prompted MSNBC commentator Eugene Robinson (2017) to remark later that same evening that fake news has become a label for "news we don't like". And Trump upped the attack the next day, calling out CNN's Senior White House correspondent as "you're fake news!" (Daily Beast, 2017), because CNN had in Trump's view reported on BuzzFeed's printing of the unverified charges with insufficient criticism. He expanded this into an all-purpose self-serving view a few weeks later, insisting that "any negative polls are fake news, just like the CNN, ABC, NBC polls in the election" (Batchelor, 2017). By the end of February 2017 and his first month as President, Trump was not only ungrammatically bellowing on Twitter that "FAKE NEWS media knowingly doesn't tell the truth" ("media" is a plural term), but barring perceived offenders CNN and *The New York Times* from White House briefings (Davis & Grynbaum, 2017). As in *The Man in the High Castle*, one man's truth is another man's poison, as fake news and real news shift in and out of focus like a classic Gestalt figure-ground diagram. (We might say that all science fiction -- for that matter, all fiction -- is fake news, except it doesn't pretend to be true.)

A further and insidious escalation of the campaign to undermine legitimate, non-fake news media -- honest, traditional journalism – was brought to light by Rachel Maddow on her MSNBC show on July 6, 2017, where she reported that her show had been shopped a cleverly concocted and nearly convincing fake news story about the Russians working with the Trump campaign during the 2016 election. The motive clearly was to erode public trust in MSNBC's reporting, and Maddow hypothesized that Dan Rather had been victimized by a similar operation when he was obliged to step down as anchor of the *CBS Evening News* in 2005 after broadcasting a story in 2004 about George W. Bush's avoidance of the draft during the Vietnam War (MacVean, 2004) -- a story based on apparently forged documents provided by sources that to this day are unclear.

These actions, caustic to the press and therefore our democracy, deserve not only condemnation but careful deconstruction. There is a significant difference, first of all, between news that we know with 100% certainty is fake -- because, as in the case of Jestin Coler, its creator tells us so, and takes us through the steps via which it was fabricated and disseminated -- and news alleged to be fake. We furthermore need to draw a distinction, as we've seen, between news that is unverified or even false, and news that is fake, since fake implies a deliberate intent to deceive. And we may need to draw clearer lines between fake news, and reporting fake news with varying degrees of identification or not of the news as fake.   The Columbia Journalism Review (Gezari, 2017) also makes a distinction between "unverified" and "unverifiable" news reports. This is important, because "unverified" implies reporting that was premature, or done by a lazy journalist, in contrast to "unverifiable," which points to deeper possible reasons for the lack of verification, which may be newsworthy in themselves.   (See also Order of the Coif, 2017, which suggests the opposite, that "unverifiable" could also mean worthy of no further investigation.)

And in effect complementing this dismissal of unwelcome news as fake news, Trump spokesperson Kellyanne Conway characterized as "alternative facts" the blatant falsehood from Press Secretary Sean Spicer that the crowd gathered for the inauguration of Donald Trump in Washington, DC "was the largest audience to ever witness an inauguration, period" (Conway, 2017).   In reality, the 1.5 million people assembled for Trump's inauguration were about a third of the number who came to see Barack Obama inaugurated in 2009 (Fandos, 2017). Thus, in this new kind of double-speak, unpleasant true news is fake news, and palpably untrue news reports are alternative facts.

Subsequent suggestions that Spicer was referring to television viewership as well as in-person attendance of Trump's inauguration are also refuted by the easily discoverable history of U. S. Presidential inauguration broadcasts, which attracted 41 million viewers for Ronald Reagan's inauguration in 1981, 38 million viewers for Barack Obama in 2009, and 33 million for Richard Nixon in 1973, in comparison to 31 million for Trump in 2017 (see Gorman, 2017, for more details).

Meanwhile, an experiment reported in 2015, but receiving little coverage in the real news media, suggests that, contrary to current concerns, people may not put that much stock or belief in fake news after all, even it agrees with their opinions. Bullock et al (2015) conducted experiments which showed that "small payments for correct and 'don't know' answers sharply diminish the gap between Democrats and Republicans in responses to 'partisan' factual questions". In other words, partisan news bubbles were punctured by even a small potential financial inducement -- correct or "don't know" answers putting respondents in a pool where they had just a one-in-a-hundred chance of winning a $200 Amazon gift certificate. Given such a motive, Democrats and Republicans by and large agreed on what was true and what was not, regardless of their political differences.

Nonetheless, whatever its ultimate impact, Facebook's much decried "algorithms" (see Hoover, 2016, and my quote in it), and their keeping track of what people read and "like" and "share" on Facebook, and feeding them more of the same, only enhances the echo chambers which Festinger and McLuhan both recognized as fundamental, ubiquitous aspects of human behavior. And this in turn has increased the concern that the combination of fake news and its ensconcing in news bubbles, free from criticism and contradicting facts, can be a toxic mix. Unsurprisingly, calls for some kind of government regulation of fake news and even Facebook have arisen. Fake news, certainly in the case of the malicious Comet Ping Pong pedophilia report, is evocative of falsely shouting fire in a crowded theater (and note the importance of "falsely" in Justice Oliver Wendell Holmes' decision -- the word is often omitted when that principle is discussed, but it's crucial, since shouting fire when there is indeed a fire could be a good thing that could save lives). But judicial "purists" and First Amendment "absolutists" -- such mid-20th century Supreme Court Justices Hugo Black and William Douglas -- have argued that "no law" means "no law" -- that the prohibition on Congress from making any law to restrict freedom of speech and press needs to be always enforced, and even the "falsely shouting fire" example fails to qualify as an utterance that Congress has a right let alone an obligation to prevent or punish if it occurs. (See my "The Flouting of the First Amendment, 2005, for why I agree.) A better way of dealing with falsely shouting fire in crowded theaters is constructing theaters with numerous, easy means of egress which defuse trampling crowds, and keeping guns out of the hands of lunatics who want to take the law into their hands on the basis of an online lie.

Further, the denunciation of unwelcome news as "fake news" by Trump and his supporters provides an unintended textbook example of why the First Amendment ought never be suspended in an attempt to extirpate fake news. Were that to happen, we would be handing someone in the White House, and his supporters, an ultimate weapon -- government prosecution and potential fine and imprisonment -- with which to eliminate any news critical of them or not to their liking.

In a significant twist to this continuing tale of falsely shouting fake news, and the need for both the non-fake news and its false identification as fake news to be protected by the First Amendment -- i.e., not shut down by the government -- we have CNN, ABC, CBS, and NBC (not Fox) refusing in May 2017 to air an ad by Trump supporters attacking those networks as purveyors of fake news. Since that ad is itself a form of fake news, or what we might call "meta-fake news", or fake news about fake news -- because those networks are not disseminating fake news -- any refusal to broadcast the ad seems like a useful step in the battle to reduce fake news. Nonetheless, Trump's daughter-in-law Lara, commenting about that refusal, observed that "mainstream media are champions of the First Amendment only when it serves their own political views" (see Hayden, 2017). That's probably true enough not only about the networks but most human beings, but since the networks are not the government, they're certainly not violating the First Amendment or any law by refusing to air a political ad that is obviously false.

But if not a violation of law, is the refusal a violation of what I like to call "the spirit of the First Amendment" (Levinson, 2010), something which occurs any time a non-governmental public agent, whether TV network or university, seeks to limit or squelch communication? Were the networks refusing to air the ad because it "doesn't fit their biased narrative," as Lara Trump also alleged (Hayden, 2017), then I think that action would indeed constitute a violation of the spirit of the First Amendment. But since the ad is demonstrably false, that surely trumps (for want of a better word) any bias that the networks might have.   The raison d'etre, again, of all forms of non-fake news reporting, including broadcasting, is to present the truth. And, surely, the elimination of fake news is integral to that mandate.

For that reason, Facebook's plan to restrict fake news by identifying phony stories in its algorithms and inserting true news stories in feeds that display fake news stories (see Hoover, 2016) is certainly a good idea, and can be seen as an attempt of Facebook to provide a new kind of gatekeeping. Of course, as in all attempts to limit hackers and other kinds of digital marauders, Facebook and the forces of truth will be involved in a constant cat-and-mouse game with the despoilers, in which every move to limit them will be sooner or later met by a technique to overcome the new barriers, and vice versa, ad infinitum.

Remedies for Fake News

The sad truth is that the very advent of fake news, whatever damage it may actually be doing, means we have to apply an adjective to news now -- true news or legitimate news -- whereas, previously, just the name "news" would do for a correct supposition by the reader, viewer, or listener that the news was true. In the end, the only reliable foundation for democracy and separation of falsity from truth, as thinkers from Jefferson to Walter Lippmann (1925) have recognized, is a well-informed public. This may be the most effective ultimate remedy for fake news, far better than government prohibition (see Zimdars, 2016, for an attempt to deal with fake news in the classroom and, by extension, the world; see also my Skype lecture, 2016a, at University of Warsaw, for more). A well-informed public would be a healthy body politic, with strong immunity to the fake news parasites that seek to invade and undermine it and us. Someday, social media may have algorithms sophisticated and intelligent enough to weed out fake news stories.

Until then:

- Humanly curated stories on Snapchat's "Discovery" and Facebook's forthcoming "Collections" insertion of curated news into its feeds are good starting points (see Tiku, 2016; Heath, 2016), which need to be buttressed by relentless public education and real news media devoting as much time to identifying fake news as reporting real news. Google's "fact-check tag," which reports to what degree a statement is confirmed as true on other sites, is also a promising start (Woollacott, 2017).
- Facebook deleted 30,000 "fake" accounts in France prior to its national election in April 2017 (Kottasová, 2017). These included not only purveyors of fake news but spam, and accounts used to artificially inflate Likes and Shares. Unfortunately, the ease with which new accounts can be created means that, as with Twitter's ongoing

battle with accounts used by ISIS and terrorists, the purging of accounts is far from a complete or even effective solution. But it's still better than doing nothing.
- Validating or verifying the accounts of people who post -- as Twitter has done for years and Facebook a little more recently with the iconic blue check mark next to the user's name -- is a time-honored, Internet-classic way of combating trolls, and presumably has reduced publishing of some fake news. In February 2017, Authenticated Reality rolled out "The New Internet," a browser overlay that allows users to verify their accounts by providing their driver's license or passport. The goal, as with the blue check mark, is to limit or eliminate fake news, online terrorists, and swindlers (Shah, 2017). But anonymity and pseudonyms (which I never favored, since I don't like talking to people with bags over their heads) has also been cited by many as a great advantage of the Internet, as an inducement to frank conversation (see "The Dark Side of New New Media" in Levinson, 2009/2013, for more on trolls and anonymity), and there's no guarantee that a validated account won't spread fake news.
- Since pursuit of advertising revenue fuels the creation and dissemination of some fake news, public denouncement of advertisements that appear on pages with fake news, and perhaps boycotts of such advertised products and services, could be a useful tool in the curbing of fake news (see Perlman, 2017).
- Seminars such as "Calling Bullshit" (Bergstrom & West, 2016), unofficially offered at the University of Washington, should be a necessary component of every college curriculum.

Approaching the problem of combatting fake news from another angle, it is crucially important that government and scientific agencies report the truth as they know it at all times. The National Weather Service's decision not to correct and reduce its forecast of a foot or two of snow in northeast big cities of the United States on March 13, 2017 because it didn't want to "confuse" the public, and wanted the public not to lesson its preparations for the predicted bigger snow fall, was a very poor decision, however well motivated, especially in this age of fake news. We always want to have complete confidence in what our government and scientific agencies tell us, but this has never been more important with so many lies masquerading as truth, and Donald Trump routinely denouncing news not to his liking as "fake". (The National Weather Service's decision is a clearer example of why the Science and Security Board of the Bulletin of the Atomic Scientists movement of the "Doomsday Clock" forward 30 seconds in 2017, mentioned earlier, was problematic.   For more on the Weather Service, see Samenow, 2017, and Levinson, 2017b.)

Meanwhile, in a notable unintended consequence, traditional newspapers are reporting a "bump" in readership in the age of fake news, Trump, and his attack on professional journalism. In a time in which everything online is understandably suspect, readers are flocking to reliable sources such as *The New York Times*, which posted a record-breaking increase of "276,000 digital news subscribers in the last quarter" of 2016 (Toonkel, 2017). And one professor of journalism, in effect adopting a Popperian approach that we learn via acquaintance with error, has argued that "truth should never be suppressed, and neither should lies, untruths or alternative facts," because "exploring these non-facts can, in reality, help us discover the truth" (Burris, 2017; see Popper, 1962, for learning from error). That's a good reason -- in addition to its violation of the First Amendment in the United States -- that fining (as the draft bill seeks to do in Germany, see Faiola & Kirchner, 2017) or criminalizing the publication of fake news on web sites is not the best solution. (Of course, the German law would have no effect in the United States, barring some kind of *Man in the High Castle* science fiction scenario., but it would establish a dangerous precedent.)

In the end, as a biological model suggests, the epidemic of fake news can best be combatted by a variety of methods, including not deliberately spreading illness (government and scientific agencies should tell the truth), washing of hands or removal of pathogens before they enter the body (curating posts and validating accounts), antibiotics (aggressive introduction of truth to combat the lies), and strengthening the immune system (education about how to recognize fake news). But just as we can never eradicate all disease-causing viruses and bacteria, we can expect to be in a never-ending battle with fake news. And just as with illness, battling fake news can sometimes make us stronger. Like illness, fake news is a part of life. And like life, the spread of fake news may have unexpected consequences.

--Paul Levinson, July 2017, New York City (first published December 2016)

Bibliography

Barry, Dan; Barstow, David; Glater, Jonathan D.; Liptak, Adam; and Steinberg, Jacques (2003) "CORRECTING THE RECORD; Times Reporter Who Resigned Leaves Long Trail of Deception," The New York Times, 11 May. http://www.nytimes.com/2003/05/11/us/correcting-the-record-times-reporter-who-resigned-leaves-long-trail-of-deception.html

Batchelor, Tom (2017) "Donald Trump: 'Negative polls are fake news'," Independent, 6 February. http://www.independent.co.uk/news/world/americas/donald-trump-negative-polls-fake-news-twitter-cnn-abc-nbc-a7564951.html

Beech, Eric (2017) "Trump calls Russia reports 'fake news - a total political witch hunt'," Reuters, 10 January. http://www.reuters.com/article/us-usa-cyber-russia-tweet-idUSKBN14V05T

Bergstrom, Carl T. & West, Jevin (2016) "Calling Bullshit In the Age of Big Data," unofficial seminar offered at University of Washington. http://callingbullshit.org/syllabus.html

Bullock, John; Gerber, Alan S.; Hill, S. J., and Huber, Gregory A. (2015) "Partisan Bias in Factual Beliefs about Politics," Quarterly Journal of Political Science, vol. 10, pp. 519–578. http://johnbullock.org/papers/partisanBiasInFactualBeliefs.pdf

Burris, Larry (2017) quoted in Baar, Aaron, "What's Search's Role In Combating Fake News?" *Media Post*, 24 January. https://www.mediapost.com/publications/article/293605/whats-searchs-role-in-combating-fake-news.html

Chozick, Amy (2016) "Hillary Clinton Blames F.B.I. Director for Election Loss," The New York Times, 12 November.

http://www.nytimes.com/2016/11/13/us/politics/hillary-clinton-james-comey.html

Clinton, Hillary (2016) "Hillary Clinton 'Fake News' Speech at the Capitol Building," Live Satellite News, YouTube, 8 December. https://www.youtube.com/watch?v=d84nRMGi7h4

Conway, Kellyanne (2017) Interview by Chuck Todd, Meet the Press, NBC-TV, 22 January. http://www.nbcnews.com/meet-the-press/video/conway-press-secretary-gave-alternative-facts-860142147643

Corera, Gordon (2017) "Cold War fake news: Why Russia lied over Aids and JFK," *BBC News*, 1 April. http://www.bbc.com/news/world-europe-39419560

Daily Beast, The (2017) "Trump Refuses to Let CNN's Jim Acosta Ask Question: 'You're Fake News!'" 11 January. http://www.thedailybeast.com/cheats/2017/01/11/jim-acosta-trump-cnn-reporter-spar-in-press-conference.html

Davis, Julie and Grynbaum, Michael (2017) "Trump Intensifies His Attacks on Journalists and Condemns F.B.I. 'Leakers'," *The New York Times*, 25 February. https://www.nytimes.com/2017/02/24/us/politics/white-house-sean-spicer-briefing.html?_r=0

Dick, Philip K. (1962) The Man in the High Castle. New York: Putnam's. Television series: Frank Spotnitz, Amazon, 2015/2016.

Dougherty, Jill (2016) "The reality behind Russia's fake news," CNN Politics, 2 December. http://www.cnn.com/2016/12/02/politics/russia-fake-news-reality/

Ellul, Jacques (1962) Propagandes. Translated by Konrad Kellen and Jean Lerneras as Propaganda: The Formation of Men's Attitudes. New York: Vintage, 1965.

Fandos, Nicholas (2017) "White House Pushes 'Alternative Facts.' Here Are the Real Ones," The New York Times, 22 January. https://www.nytimes.com/2017/01/22/us/politics/president-trump-inauguration-crowd-white-house.html

Faiola, Anthony & Kirchner, Stephanie (2017) "How do you stop fake news? In Germany, with a law," *Washington Post*, 5 April. https://www.washingtonpost.com/world/europe/how-do-you-stop-fake-news-in-germany-with-a-law/2017/04/05/e6834ad6-1a08-11e7-bcc2-7d1a0973e7b2_story.html

Farnsworth, Meghann (2017) "Live now: Watch Hillary Clinton from our Code Conference," *recode*, 31 May. https://www.recode.net/2017/5/31/15716226/watch-live-hillary-clinton-code-conference-today

Festinger, Leon (1957) A Theory of Cognitive Dissonance. Stanford, CA: Stanford University Press.

Fifield, Anna (2017) "Blaming 'fake news,' Ban Ki-moon drops presidential bid in South Korea," Washington Post, 1 February. https://www.washingtonpost.com/world/former-un-chief-ban-ki-moon-will-not-run-for-president-of-south-korea/2017/02/01/b05c816d-9ce5-4c3a-84be-0e5b78890a17_story.html

Gernsback, Hugo (1926) "The Moon Hoax," Amazing Stories, September. Discussed in Wythoff (2016).

Gezari, Vanessa M. (2017) "BuzzFeed was right to publish Trump-Russia files," Columbia Journalism Review, 11 January. http://www.cjr.org/criticism/buzzfeed_trump_russia_memos.php

Giles, Jim (2005) "Special report: Internet encyclopaedias go head-to-head," Nature, 14 December.
http://www.nature.com/nature/journal/v438/n7070/full/438900a.html

Gillin, Joshua (2016) "How Pizzagate went from fake news to a real problem for a D.C. business," POLITIFACT, 5 December.
http://www.politifact.com/truth-o-meter/article/2016/dec/05/how-pizzagate-went-fake-news-real-problem-dc-busin/

Gorman, Steve (2017) "Trump inauguration draws nearly 31 million U.S. television viewers," Reuters, 22 January.
http://www.reuters.com/article/us-usa-trump-inauguration-ratings-idUSKBN15600S

Harmon, Amy (2003) "'I Now Inform You'," The New York Times, 18 May.
http://www.nytimes.com/2003/05/18/weekinreview/i-now-inform-you.html

Hart, William; Albarracín, Dolores; Eagly, Alice H.; Brechan, Inge; Lindberg, Matthew J. & Merrill, Lisa (2009) "Feeling validated versus being correct: A meta-analysis of selective exposure to information," Psychological Bulletin, 135/4, July.

Hayden, Eric (2017) "Trump's 'Fake News' Ad Refused by More Major TV Networks," *The Hollywood Reporter*, 5 May.
http://www.hollywoodreporter.com/news/more-major-networks-refuse-trumps-fake-news-ad-1000615

Heath, Alex (2016) "Facebook working on a plan to pick news from favored media partners like Snapchat," Business Insider, 2 December.
http://www.businessinsider.com/facebook-working-on-curated-collections-section-for-news-feed-with-publishers-2016-12

Hoover, Amanda (2016) "How curated articles could help Facebook fight fake news," Christian Science Monitor, 4 December.
http://www.csmonitor.com/Technology/2016/1204/How-curated-articles-could-help-Facebook-fight-fake-news

Kottasová, Ivana (2017) "Facebook targets 30,000 fake accounts in France," *CNN Media*, 21 April.
http://money.cnn.com/2017/04/14/media/facebook-fake-news-france-election/

Lee, Alfred McClung and Lee, Elizabeth Briant (1939) The Fine Art of Propaganda. New York: Harcourt Brace.

Lee, Timothy B. (2016) "The top 20 fake news stories outperformed real news at the end of the 2016 campaign," Vox, 16 November.
http://www.vox.com/new-money/2016/11/16/13659840/facebook-fake-news-chart

Levinson, Paul (2005) "The Flouting of the First Amendment," Keynote Address, Sixth Annual Convention of the Media Ecology Association, Fordham University, New York City, 23 June.
transcript: http://paullevinson.blogspot.com/2007/07/flouting-of-first-amendment-transcript.html
video: https://www.youtube.com/watch?v=qXwcC0MTME8

____ (2009/2013) New New Media. New York: Pearson.

____ (2010) "Blagojevich and Fair Trial 1, Fitzgerald 0," *Infinite Regress* blog, 10 April.
http://paullevinson.blogspot.com/2010/08/blagojevich-and-fair-trial-1-fitzgerald.html

____ (2015/2016) McLuhan in an Age of Social Media. New York: Connected Editions

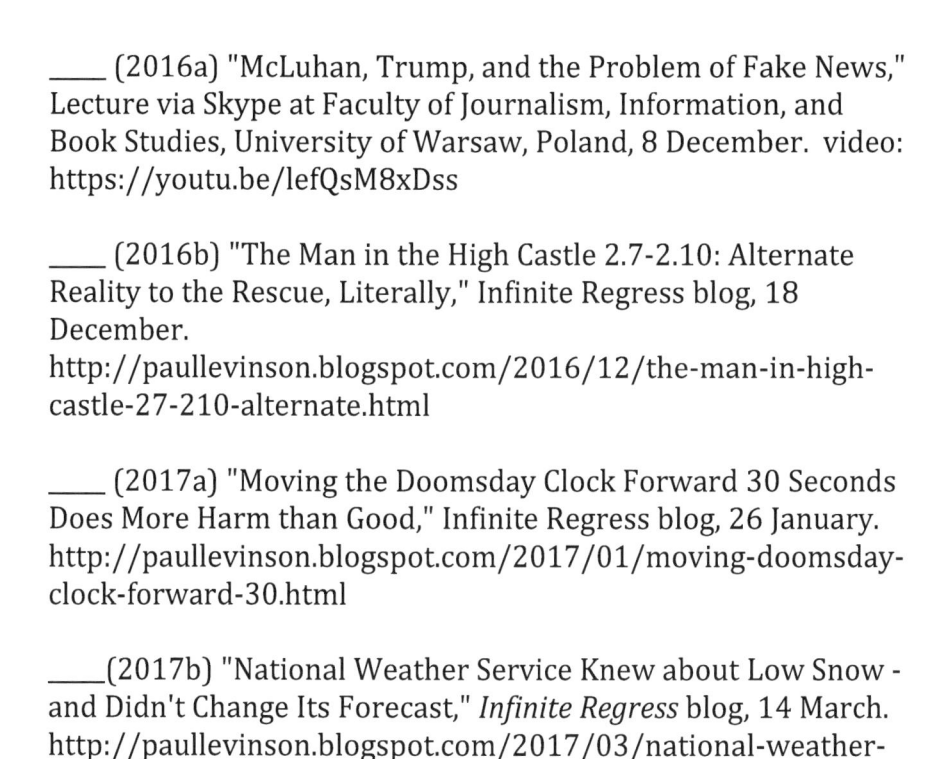

____ (2016a) "McLuhan, Trump, and the Problem of Fake News," Lecture via Skype at Faculty of Journalism, Information, and Book Studies, University of Warsaw, Poland, 8 December. video: https://youtu.be/lefQsM8xDss

____ (2016b) "The Man in the High Castle 2.7-2.10: Alternate Reality to the Rescue, Literally," Infinite Regress blog, 18 December. http://paullevinson.blogspot.com/2016/12/the-man-in-high-castle-27-210-alternate.html

____ (2017a) "Moving the Doomsday Clock Forward 30 Seconds Does More Harm than Good," Infinite Regress blog, 26 January. http://paullevinson.blogspot.com/2017/01/moving-doomsday-clock-forward-30.html

____(2017b) "National Weather Service Knew about Low Snow - and Didn't Change Its Forecast," *Infinite Regress* blog, 14 March. http://paullevinson.blogspot.com/2017/03/national-weather-service-knew-about-low.html

Lippmann, Walter (1925) The Phantom Public. New York: Macmillan.

Livingston, Michael (2016) Comment on David Itzkoff's "How 'Rogue One' Brought Back Familiar Faces," The New York Times, 27 December (comment made 9:22am). http://mobile.nytimes.com/comments/2016/12/27/movies/how-rogue-one-brought-back-grand-moff-tarkin.html

MacVean, Mary (2004) "Dan Rather to Quit 'CBS Evening News'," *Los Angeles Times*, 23 November. http://www.latimes.com/la-112304rather_lat-story.html

Maddow, Rachel (2017) *The Rachel Maddow Show*, MSNBC, 6 July 2017

McLuhan, Marshall (1964) Understanding Media. New York: Mentor

____ (1970) Culture Is Our Business. New York: McGraw-Hill.

____ (1977) "The Laws of the Media," Preface by Paul Levinson, et cetera (34) 2, pp. 173–179.

Metropolitan Museum of Art (2012) "Faking It: Manipulated Photography Before Photoshop," 11 October. http://www.metmuseum.org/exhibitions/listings/2012/faking-it

Order of the Coif (2017) "Buzzfeed and the Manchurian Candidate," 12 January. https://orderofthecoif.wordpress.com/2017/01/12/buzzfeed-and-the-manchurian-candidate/

Perlman, Elisabeth (2017) "Fool's gold: Remove the financial incentive of fake news," *Verdict*, 15 February. http://www.verdict.co.uk/fools-gold-remove-financial-incentive-fake-news

Percival, Ray Scott (2011) *The Myth of the Closed Mind*. Chicago, IL: Open Court.

Popper, Karl (1945) The Open Society and Its Enemies. London: Routledge.

____ (1962) *Conjectures and Refutations*. London: Routledge.

Reilly, Patrick (2017) "Research shows how to 'inoculate' readers from fake news," The Christian Science Monitor, 24 January. http://www.csmonitor.com/Technology/2017/0124/Research-shows-how-to-innoculate-readers-from-fake-news

Robinson, Eugene (2017) Commentary made on The 11th Hour with Brian Williams, MSNBC TV, 10 January.

Samenow, Jason (2017) "Weather Service made poor decision in overplaying Nor'easter snow predictions," *Washington Post*, 15 March. https://www.washingtonpost.com/news/capital-weather-gang/wp/2017/03/15/weather-service-made-poor-decision-in-overplaying-noreaster-snow-predictions/?utm_term=.2eb014f08266

Science and Security Board (2017) "It is two and a half minutes to midnight: 2017 Doomsday Clock Statement," Bulletin of the Atomic Scientists, 26 January. https://thebulletin.org/sites/default/files/Final%202017%20Clock%20Statement.pdf

Selwyn-Holmes, Alex (2010) "Lincoln-Calhoun Composite," Iconic Photos, 24 April. https://iconicphotos.wordpress.com/2010/04/24/lincoln-calhoun-composite/

Shah, Angela (2017) "Amid Fake News, Authenticated Reality Launches 'The New Internet'," *Xconomy*, 13 February. http://www.xconomy.com/texas/2017/02/13/amid-fake-news-authenticated-reality-launches-the-new-internet

Smith, Alexander and Banic, Vladimir (2016) "Fake News: How a Partying Macedonian Teen Earns Thousands Publishing Lies," NBC News, 9 December. http://www.nbcnews.com/news/world/fake-news-how-partying-macedonian-teen-earns-thousands-publishing-lies-n692451

Smith, Gerry (2016) "HGTV Will Never Upset You: How the Network Beat CNN in 2016," Bloomberg, 28 December. https://www.bloomberg.com/news/articles/2016-12-28/hgtv-will-never-upset-you-how-the-network-beat-cnn-in-2016

Soboroff, Jacob (2016) Interview of Jestin Coler, The 11th Hour with Brian Williams, MSNBC, 5 December. http://www.msnbc.com/brian-williams/watch/exclusive-interview-with-man-behind-fake-campaign-news-825635395578

Soll, Jacob (2016) "The Long and Brutal History of Fake News," Politico Magazine, 18 December. http://www.politico.com/magazine/story/2016/12/fake-news-history-long-violent-214535

Stone, Peter & Gordon, Greg (2017) "Trump-Russia investigators probe Jared Kushner-run digital operation," *McClatchy DC Bureau*, 11 July. http://www.mcclatchydc.com/news/nation-world/national/article160803619.html

Tedford, Thomas L. and Herbeck, Dale A. Freedom of Speech in the United States, 7th edition. State College, PA: Strata.

Tiku, Nitasha (2016) "Why Snapchat And Apple Don't Have A Fake News Problem," Buzzfeed News, 1 December. https://www.buzzfeed.com/nitashatiku/snapchat-fake-news

Toonkel, Jessica (2017) "Newspapers aim to ride 'Trump Bump' to reach readers, advertisers," *Reuters, Data Dive*, 16 February. http://www.reuters.com/article/us-newspapers-trump-campaigns-analysis-idUSKBN15V0GI

Welles, Orson (1938) "The War of the Worlds," The Mercury Theater on the Air, CBS Radio, 30 October.

Woollacott, Emma (2017) "Google Brings 'Fact Check' Tag To Search Results," *Forbes*, 7 April. https://www.forbes.com/sites/emmawoollacott/2017/04/07/google-brings-fact-check-tag-to-search-results/#1208b6a86109

Wythoff, Grant, ed. (2016) The Perversity of Things: Hugo Gernsback on Media, Tinkering, and Scientifiction. Minneapolis, MN: University of Minnesota Press.

Zimdars, Melissa (2016) "My 'fake news list' went viral. But made-up stories are only part of the problem," Washington Post, 18 November. https://www.washingtonpost.com/posteverything/wp/2016/11/18/my-fake-news-list-went-viral-but-made-up-stories-are-only-part-of-the-problem

About the Author

Paul Levinson, PhD, is Professor of Communication & Media Studies at Fordham University in NYC. His nonfiction books, including The Soft Edge (1997), Digital McLuhan (1999), Realspace (2003), Cellphone (2004), and New New Media (2009; 2nd edition, 2012), have been translated into fifteen languages. His science fiction novels include The Silk Code (winner of Locus Award for Best First Science Fiction Novel of 1999), Borrowed Tides (2001), The Consciousness Plague (2002), The Pixel Eye (2003), The Plot To Save Socrates (2006), Unburning Alexandria (2013), and Chronica (2014) -- the last three of which are also known as the Sierra Waters trilogy, and are historical as well as science fiction. He appears on CNN, MSNBC, Fox News, the Discovery Channel, National Geographic, the History Channel, NPR, and numerous TV and radio programs. His 1972 LP, Twice Upon a Rhyme, was re-issued in 2010. He reviews television in his InfiniteRegress.tv blog, and was listed in The Chronicle of Higher Education's "Top 10 Academic Twitterers" in 2009.

The following books by Paul Levinson available in print and Kindle:

Nonfiction:

The Soft Edge: A Natural History and Future of the Information Revolution

Digital McLuhan: A Guide to the Information Millennium

McLuhan in an Age of Social Media

Realspace: The Fate of Physical Presence in the Digital Age, On and Off Planet

New New Media

From Media Theory to Space Odyssey: Petar Jandrić interviews Paul Levinson

Cyber War and Peace

Science fiction:

Loose Ends (time travel) series (complete):
Loose Ends, Little Differences, Late Lessons, Last Calls

Sierra Waters (time travel) series:
The Plot to Save Socrates, Unburning Alexandria, Chronica

Phil D'Amato forensic detective series:
The Chronology Protection Case, The Silk Code, The Consciousness Plague, The Pixel Eye

Ian's Ions and Eons (three time travel novelettes)

Exo-Genetic Engineers series:
The Orchard, The Suspended Fourth

Borrowed Tides

Double Realities series:
The Other Car, Extra Credit, The Wallet

The Kid in the Video Store

Nonfiction and Science Fiction

Touching the Face of the Cosmos: On the Intersection of Space Travel and Religion

Follow Paul Levinson at Twitter: @PaulLev

Printed in Great Britain
by Amazon